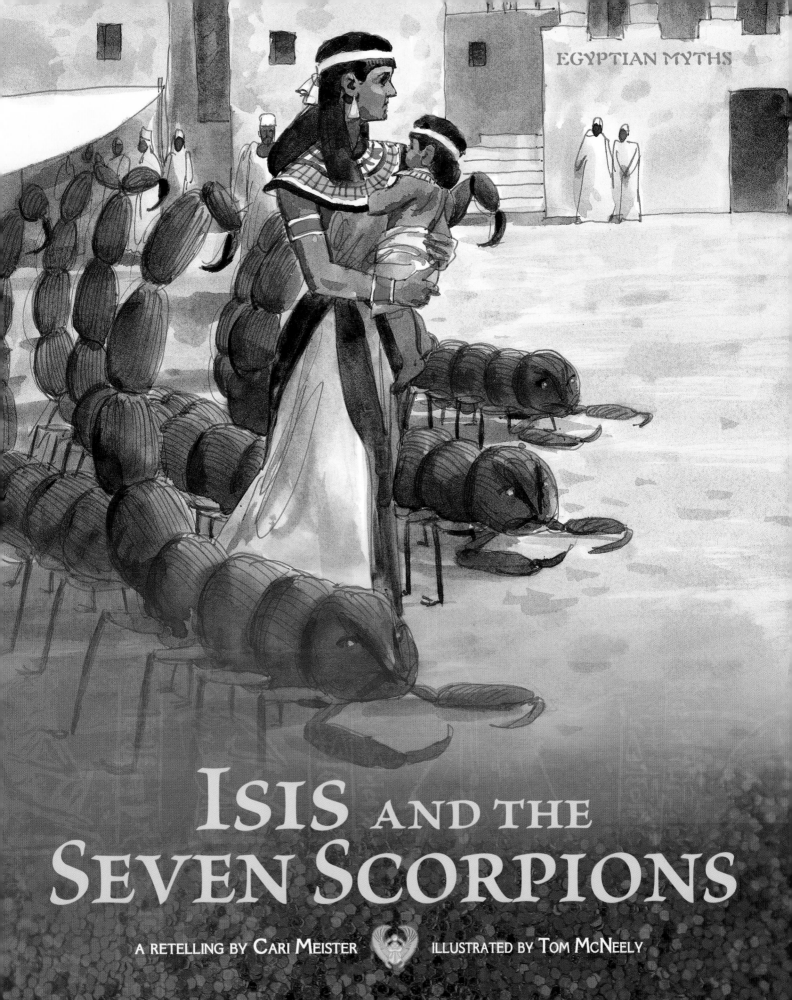

EGYPTIAN MYTHS

ISIS AND THE SEVEN SCORPIONS

A RETELLING BY CARI MEISTER   ILLUSTRATED BY TOM MCNEELY

PICTURE WINDOW BOOKS
a capstone imprint

CAST OF CHARACTERS

Osiris (oh-SIRE-is): god of the underworld; brother of Isis and Set; husband of Isis

Set (SET): god of the desert and storms; brother of Isis and Osiris

Isis (EYE-sis): goddess of magic and life; sister of Osiris and Set; wife of Osiris

Horus (HOAR-us): god of the sky; son of Isis and Osiris

Thoth (THOTH): god of wisdom

The seven scorpions:

Petet (pet-ET)

Tjetet (jet-ET)

Matet (MET)

Mesetet (mez-uh-TET)

Mesetetef (mess-ET-aif)

Tefen (TE-fen)

Befen (BUH-fen)

 # WORDS TO KNOW

flank—to be posted at the side of

myth—a story told by people in ancient times; myths often tried to explain natural events

papyrus—a tall water plant that grows in northern Africa and southern Europe; a material that is written on can be made from the stems of this plant

shroud—cloth that is used to wrap a dead body

venom—a poisonous liquid produced by some animals

IN ONE ANCIENT EGYPTIAN MYTH, the god Osiris is murdered by his brother Set. Set murdered Osiris so he could rule Egypt.

Osiris' wife, Isis, wanted to give her husband a proper burial. After his death, she weaved shrouds of linen to wrap around his body.

Set provided a special weaving room in the palace for Isis. After all, he wanted to keep a close eye on her and Osiris' young son, Horus.

In the guarded weaving room, Isis spent day after day weaving linen strips. She rarely let Horus out of her sight, because she was afraid Set would kill him too. But the god of wisdom, Thoth, had a plan to protect Isis and Horus from the evil Set.

Isis was in the weaving room when a giant sandstorm came in from the desert.

She quickly rose from the floor and closed the windows. "Hurry, Horus!" she said to her little child. "Come here."

Isis wrapped Horus in a blanket. When she looked up, the god of wisdom, Thoth, had appeared in the room.

"How did you get past the guards?" Isis asked Thoth.

Thoth pointed to the storm he had created. "Dust hides many things," he said.

Isis nodded at the clever god. She knew he was here for a reason.

"You must leave the palace tonight," Thoth said. "Set plans to kill Horus. The storm will make it easier for you to escape. We cannot trust the guards to take you. So I have created seven giant magical scorpions to help you. Their names are Petet, Tjetet, Matet, Mesetet, Mesetetef, Tefen, and Befen. It is very important that you remember their names. Saying their names gives you the power to control them. The scorpions will arrive tonight."

Before Isis could ask any more questions, Thoth disappeared in a cloud of dust.

That night the seven giant scorpions appeared in the weaving room. It was time to escape.

"We are ready," said Isis.

The scorpions bowed before the goddess and her son. Then the scorpions guided them out of the palace.

Three of the scorpions—Petet, Tjetet, and Matet—went in front. The scorpions Mesetet and Mesetetef flanked Isis' sides. Tefen and Befen followed Isis.

The sandstorm was still in full force. The dust was so thick that the guards did not see them escape.

The group traveled throughout the night, following the papyrus swamps. Isis told the scorpions not to talk to anyone. "Set must not find out which way we went," she said.

They walked many miles. By the next afternoon, Isis was tired and longed to rest. As they approached the town of Two Sisters, Horus began to cry. He was hungry and did not want to travel anymore.

"Okay, my son," Isis said, "we will stop here for the night. Surely the fine people of this town will give us a comfortable place to stay."

As they entered the town, Isis spotted a large house. "I will ask these kind people for help."

Isis knocked on the door. A servant girl answered. "We have been traveling all night and day," Isis told her. "Would you please let us rest for the night? Do not fear the scorpions; they are here to protect us."

The servant girl went to find her mistress. It was not long before the mistress was at the door. When she saw the group, her eyes widened. "How dare you come to my house! Be gone quickly, before anyone sees you standing here!"

But it was too late. Everyone in the town had seen the group walking. Now everyone watched as the rude noblewoman yelled and sent away Isis and her child.

13

Horus started to cry again. "Hush, hush," said Isis to her child. "We will find someone with a kind heart."

They barely left the walkway of the large house, when a woman dressed in rags appeared.

"I see you are tired and hungry," the woman said. "You can come stay at my house. It is not much, but it is a place to eat and rest."

"Thank you," said Isis. "We would welcome the chance to share your home."

Isis and Horus followed the woman to her small home. They ate and were soon resting peacefully.

The scorpions, on the other hand, were furious. "How dare that rich women yell at us!" said Petet.

"How dare she refuse Isis and Horus a place to stay!" said Tjetet.

"She should be punished!" said Matet.

"I have an idea," said Tefen. "Load all of your venom into me, and I will shrink down to normal size. Then I will go under the door of the rich woman's house and sting her son. Surely all of our venom together will kill him. Then she will be sorry!"

All the scorpions agreed that it was a great plan.

17

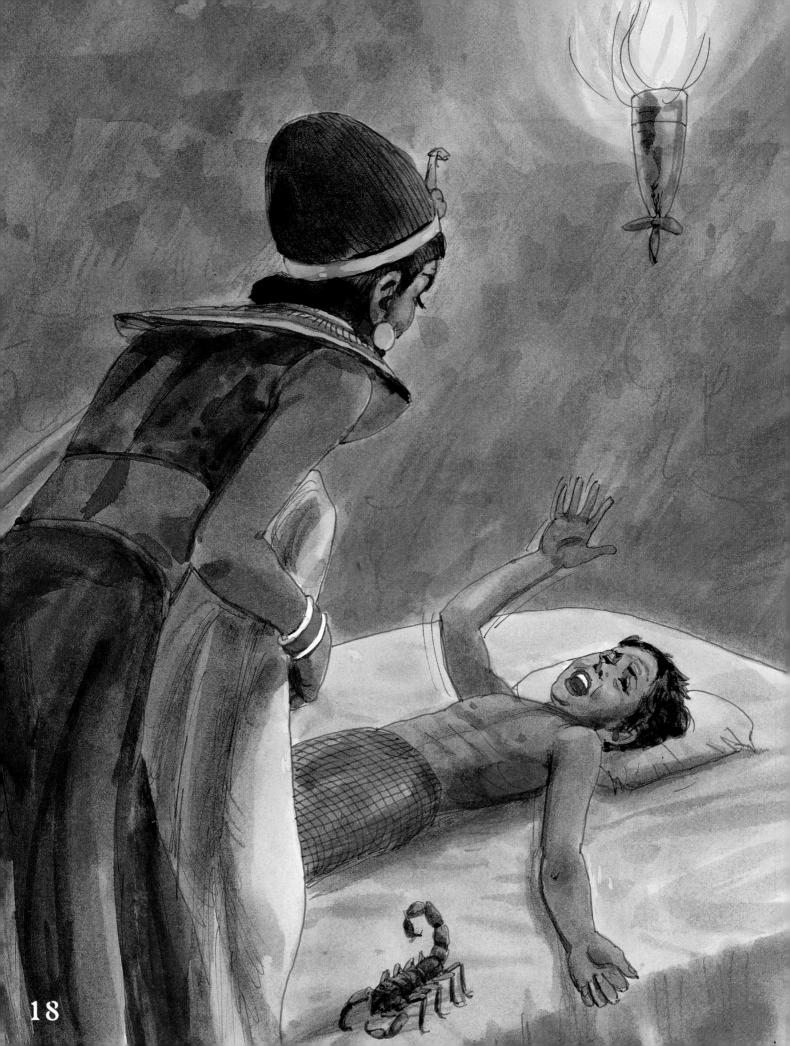

Early the next morning, loaded with six times his normal venom, Tefen snuck under the door of the large house. He scurried in and out of rooms until he found the young son's bed.

Tefen crawled under the covers and injected all the venom into the boy.

"Mama! Mama!" the boy screamed.

His mother ran into the room and saw her son thrashing around violently. Then she looked down. "A scorpion!" she screamed. "Gods, please help him!"

The woman grabbed her son and ran into the street, screaming, "Please help me! My son was stung by a scorpion! He is near death!"

But her cries were in vain. The village people had seen how the woman had treated Isis and Horus when they were in need. Now every door was closed in her face.

"Serves her right!" said one villager.

"She doesn't deserve a son, anyway," said another.

The woman's cries woke Isis, who quickly dressed and ran out to meet her.

21

"The poor boy!" said Isis when she saw him. "I must help him!"

"But that woman was so rude to you!" said Befen.

"We did this to the boy," said Tjetet. "We wanted to seek revenge for you."

"She deserves this fate," said Matet.

But Isis was angry with them. "No mother deserves to lose her son to revenge!" she said. "Quickly, we must help him. Go get some barley bread, garlic, and salt. Rub these things all over the boy."

By this time, the boy looked like death. Everybody knew that he was beyond saving.

Isis, the goddess of magic, knew she could save him if she revealed her true goddess self. "City of Two Sisters," she told the crowd that had gathered, "I am the goddess Isis. I can save this boy because Thoth told me the scorpions' secret names. Because I know their names, I can make their venom harmless. However, you must not tell anyone of my deed until my son, Horus, becomes ruler of Egypt."

26

The crowd agreed and watched in awe as Isis changed into her true goddess form.

She quietly chanted a spell and called each scorpion by name. "Petet, Tjetet, Matet, Mesetet, Mesetetef, Tefen, and Befen."

The venom in the boy lost its power. He regained his color and coughed. "Mama!" he cried as he clung to his mother.

The woman bowed before Isis and said, "Great goddess, Isis. Please forgive me for my rude behavior. You are kind and good, and you saved my son. I am forever grateful. I wish for you to have all of my possessions—my house, my jewels, and my servants."

Isis smiled down at the woman and said, "You are forgiven. Thank you for the offer of your possessions, but I do not need them. However, the kind woman I stayed with last night could use your generosity."

"Of course!" said the woman. She showered the poor woman with riches for the rest of her life.

Isis, Horus, and the scorpions traveled along the banks of the Nile River for many years. Finally Horus was old enough and strong enough to challenge his uncle Set for the throne.

The scorpions were sorry for what they had done to the boy. They remained faithful to Isis forever.

READ MORE

Adamson, Heather. *Ancient Egypt: An Interactive History Adventure.* You Choose Books. Mankato, Minn.: Capstone Press, 2010.

Bell, Michael, and Sarah Quie. *Ancient Egyptian Civilization.* Ancient Civilizations and Their Myths and Legends. New York: Rosen Central, 2010.

Elgin, Kathy. *Egyptian Myths.* Myths From Many Lands. New York: Skyview Books, 2009.

INTERNET SITES

FactHound offers a safe, fun way to find Internet sites related to this book. All of the sites on FactHound have been researched by our staff.

Here's all you do:

Visit *www.facthound.com*

Type in this code: 9781404871502

Check out projects, games and lots more at
www.capstonekids.com

LOOK FOR ALL THE BOOKS IN THE EGYPTIAN MYTHS SERIES:

ISIS AND OSIRIS

ISIS AND THE SEVEN SCORPIONS

THE PRINCE AND THE SPHINX

THE SEARCH FOR THE BOOK OF THOTH

Thanks to our adviser for his expertise and advice:
Terry Flaherty, PhD
Professor of English
Minnesota State University, Mankato

Editor: Shelly Lyons
Designer: Ted Williams
Art Director: Nathan Gassman
Production Specialist: Danielle Ceminsky
The illustrations in this book were created with watercolors, gouache, acrylics, and digitally.
Artistic Effects
Shutterstock: Goran Bogicevic, Kristina Divinchuk, Shvaygert Ekaterina, Vladislav Gurfinkel

Picture Window Books
1710 Roe Crest Drive
North Mankato, MN 56003
www.capstonepub.com

All books published by Picture Window Books are manufactured with paper containing at least 10 percent post-consumer waste.

Library of Congress Cataloging-in-Publication Data
Meister, Cari.
 Isis and the seven scorpions : a retelling / by Cari Meister ; illustrated by Tom McNeely.
    p. cm. — (Egyptian myths)
 "A Capstone imprint."
 ISBN 978-1-4048-7150-2 (library binding)
 ISBN 978-1-4048-7241-7 (paperback)
 1. Gods, Egyptian—Juvenile literature. 2. Goddesses, Egyptian—Juvenile literature. 3. Mythology, Egyptian—Juvenile literature. I. McNeely, Tom. II. Title. III. Series: Egyptian myths.
 BL2450.G6M455 2012
 299.3113—dc23
                                     2011025841

Printed in the United States of America in Stevens Point, Wisconsin.
102011   006404WZS12